The History of Lucy®

The World's Largest Elephant

...and America's Oldest Roadside Attraction!

A National Historic Landmark

By William McMahon

COMTEQ PUBLISHING
MARGATE, NEW JERSEY

Copyright © 1988, 2009 by Save Lucy Committee, Inc., Margate, NJ

All rights reserved. No part of this book may be used or reproduced in any manner, electronic or mechanical, including photocopying, recording or by any information storage and retrieval system, or otherwise, without written permission from the publisher.

Published by:
    ComteQ Publishing
    A division of ComteQ Communications, LLC
    Margate, NJ
    609-487-9000
    Website: www.ComteQpublishing.com

ISBN 978-1-935232-06-3
Library of Congress Control Number: 2009931541

Book and cover design by Rob Huberman
Cover photo by Larry Sieg, Atlantic City Convention & Visitors Authority

Printed in the United States of America

Lucy's Vital Statistics

Lucy The Elephant stands in a feeding position, trunk down. Access to her interior is gained through spiral stairways in the hind legs, one being for the entrance and the other the exit. Entrance stairs lead to a reception room, which is 18 by 18 feet. Other rooms are off this main one. There are 17 windows.

In the construction of this giant made of wood and metal, it is said that a million pieces of timber and 8,560 ribs or arches, 200 kegs of nails, and four tons of bolts and bars were used. It required 12,000 square feet of tin to cover the structure.

The body is 38 feet long and 80 feet in circumference; the head is 16 feet long and 48 feet in circumference. Lucy's neck is six feet long and 48 feet in circumference; legs are 22 feet long and 10 feet in diameter. The ears are 17 feet long and 10 feet wide. It is estimated that each weighs 2,000 pounds.

Lucy's tusks are 22 feet long; tail 26 feet and glass window eyes are 18 inches in diameter.

It is estimated that Lucy can be seen (without use of binoculars) from up to eight miles away.

Lucy in the 1990s.

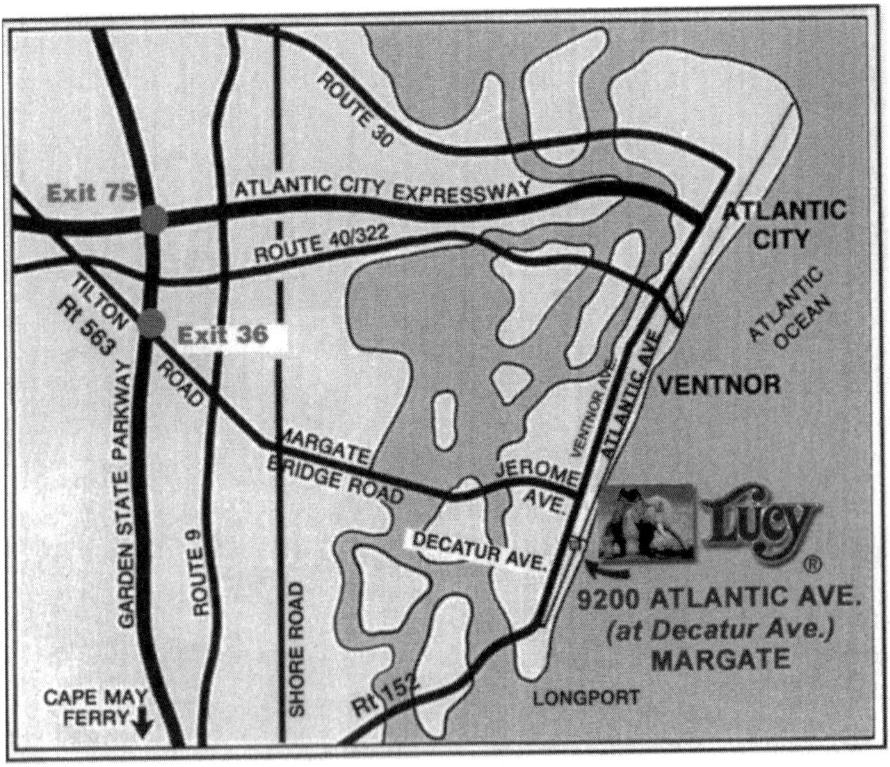
ROUTE 30
Exit 7S
ATLANTIC CITY EXPRESSWAY
ATLANTIC CITY
ROUTE 40/322
TILTON Rt 563
Exit 36
ROAD
ATLANTIC OCEAN
VENTNOR
GARDEN STATE PARKWAY
MARGATE BRIDGE ROAD
JEROME AVE.
VENTNOR AVE.
ATLANTIC AVE
Lucy®
DECATUR AVE.
ROUTE 9
SHORE ROAD
9200 ATLANTIC AVE.
(at Decatur Ave.)
MARGATE
CAPE MAY FERRY
Rt 152
LONGPORT

The 1800s: Elephant to Starboard!

The outer islands of the Southern Jersey coast are romantically entwined with legends of pirate chieftains fighting battles to the death on sandy beaches, of buried treasure beneath every dune and of whalers rushing for boats when the cry of "Thar' She Blows" echoed from lookout stations.

Mysterious cargoes landed in the dead of night and were quickly gathered by horsemen who disappeared in the deep shadows of the pines, according to legend. Pages of the past are so cluttered with this type of adventure that even dedicated historians are hard pressed to separate fact from fiction.

However, no legend of the colorful Southern Jersey seashore history matches the sight of a 65-foot high wooden elephant astride the beach looking out into the mists of the sea, a spectacle that according to historians, made many coastwise seamen of the tramp ships from the West Indies swear off their rum rations for days.

There is the story of one young seaman on his first voyage who had the early evening watch as his ship made it up the coast on its way to New York harbor.

After first reporting, "All's well" he suddenly yelled, "Elephant!"

The captain, thinking the seaman had gone beserk, rushed to the deck. Lifting his long glass to the shoreline he also exclaimed "Elephant!" and wiped off his glass. After a second look, he confirmed the fact that there was a giant beast standing among the dunes and eel grass of lower Absecon Island.

The captain's report at anchoring in New York harbor brought a score of newspeople and the curious southward into New Jersey to investigate.

Lucy the Elephant as she appeared about 1885.

James V. Lafferty, Jr. and children. Believed to be the only photograph.

After a long, dusty ride from the upper part of Absecon Island to what was then called South Atlantic City, the investigators found that the elephant was no mirage. Here it stood in full majesty, king of all it surveyed.

Metropolitan newspapers the next day were telling the story of a wooden elephant, which later would become known as "Lucy," much to the delight of land speculator James V. Lafferty, Jr., who was responsible for the designing and building of the strange pachyderm.

James Vincent de Paul Lafferty, Jr. was born in Philadelphia, Pa. in 1856, of prosperous Irish immigrant parents from Dublin. Lafferty and his wife Mary Cecelia Tobin had five children, two of whom died in their childhood. Surviving were Mazie, James III and the youngest son Robert.

Lafferty, who grew up to be an engineer and inventor, came into possession of a number of sandy lots in the South Atlantic City area. They were cut off from the frame houses and mule-drawn street cars of Atlantic City by a deep tidal creek. Only at low tide could anyone make his way down to the sands of his properties.

Most of South Atlantic City at that time was a combination of scrub pine, dune grass, bayberry bushes and a few wooden fishing shacks.

Once Lafferty hit upon the elephant idea he enlisted the aid of a Philadelphia architect named William Free to design this unusual structure that he felt would attract visitors and property buyers to his holdings.

The elephant was constructed in 1881 by a Philadelphia contractor at a reported cost of $25,000, which at the time was a considerable amount of money. Lafferty always claimed that before the work was finished, the cost had sky-rocketed to $38,000.

To protect his original idea, Lafferty applied for and received a patent from the U.S. Government. He made his original application June 3, 1882 and received patent No. 268-503 on Dec. 5, 1882.

In his application Lafferty stated: "My invention consists of a building in the form of an animal, the body of which is floored and divided into rooms... the legs contain the stairs which lead to the body..."

Lafferty also included a paragraph that stated the building "may be in the form of any other animal than an elephant, as that of a fish, fowl, etc." What his intentions were in adding that paragraph have never been clear. He never attempted a building in any of the forms mentioned.

It is believed that most of the materials were brought to the site by boat, although there was rail service of a sort in the upper part of Absecon Island where the nacient resort of Atlantic City was just getting underway.

By 1881 Lafferty was placing advertisements in area and Philadelphia newspapers offering building lots in "fast booming South Atlantic City."

Lafferty eventually extended himself too far in his land deals both at the Jersey Shore and in New York and by 1887 sought to unload his South Atlantic City holdings. He offered the elephant and other property for sale and found a willing buyer in Anton Gertzen of Philadelphia.

Lafferty died in 1898 and is buried in the family vault in the cemetery of St. Augustine's Catholic Church, one of Philadelphia's oldest churches (1796), which still stands in the shadow of the Benjamin Franklin Bridge.

South Atlantic City: Now Margate City

To avoid any confusion to readers following the history of Lucy from South Atlantic City to Margate City, it might be well to note that both are the same community. What is now Margate City was originally a part of Egg Harbor Township, but its citizens broke from the township on August 4, 1885 and organized the Borough of South Atlantic City. On April 23, 1897 it was re-incorporated as the City of South Atlantic City and on April 20, 1909 the name was changed to Margate City, after a famous resort in England. James Rider was the first mayor of the community and lived to the ripe age of 105.

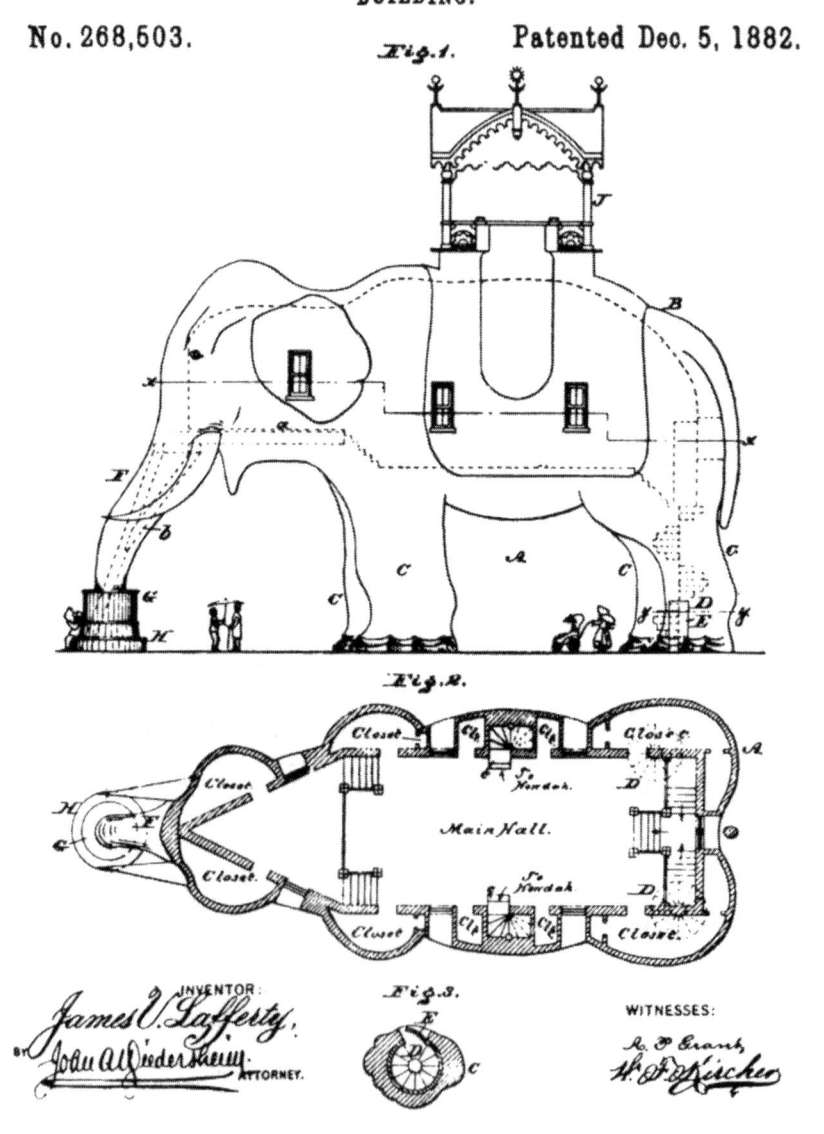

Full page Drawings for Lafferty Patent.

The 1800s: The Gertzen Family Buys Lucy

The Gertzens, who were to play a prominent part in the early history of both Lucy the Elephant and South Atlantic City, were an interesting family.

Anton Gertzen, the patriarch of the family, was born in 1823 in the German State of Prussia, which is now part of the Federal Republic of Germany.

In 1844 Anton left his native land for the United States and settled in Philadelphia where he met Caroline Schurmann. Oddly enough, both had crossed the Atlantic Ocean in the same ship but had not met aboard.

Caroline, daughter of Dominicus Schurmann and Dorothea Webber Schurmann, was one of eight children born in Rotterdam, Holland. Anton, who had changed his name to Anthony, and Caroline were wed in St. Mary's Catholic Church in Philadelphia.

During the years they had seven children: Anthony, Jr., Henry F., John, Ignatius, Caroline, Ann-Catherine and Josephine.

On a visit to South Atlantic City, Anthony, who loved sports fishing, was impressed by the community as a future home. He began to spend more and more time at the seashore and finally settled after buying various parcels

Fishermen's Hotel long a part of the Margate scene owned by Henry Gertzen who also operated a fleet of fishing vessels.

of land and going into the fishing boat business. Lucy the Elephant was one of his purchases.

Anthony Sr., died in 1902. All of the properties he had acquired including the fishing business were divided among his children.

Anthony Jr. expanded the investments and served for many years as City Clerk of Margate. He had one son, Anthony III.

Henry F., the second son of Anthony and Caroline, was born in 1849 and participated in the family carpet business. He also moved to South Atlantic City and served as mayor of the town for eighteen years. He is credited with the selection of the Independence Hall of Philadelphia as the architectural model for the new city hall of Margate City.

Henry F. also operated the Gables Hotel and fishing fleet of 100 boats as well as Fishermen's Hotel. All were located near Washington and Amherst Avenues. Henry F. died in 1933 at the age of 84.

John Gertzen, the third son, married Sophia Blackowski and they had three children: Caroline, John, and Joseph F.

Margate City Hall, designed by Henry Gertzen along the same lines as Independence Hall in Philadelphia. It was built in 1903 and today remains the site of all Margate City municipal offices and commission chambers.

John and Sophia Gertzen. Gertzen figured prominently in the history of Lucy the Elephant and owned the structure from the time Lafferty bowed out and up until the Save Lucy Committee took over in 1970.

Caroline Mae Gertzen about 1903 from Hattie Pfeil's scrapbook.

John purchased the six-story elephant structure and other properties from his mother, thus continuing a long family history of connection with the elephant building.

Gertzen charged visitors 10¢ to tour the furnished interior of the elephant building and climb the spiral stairway to the howdah, or observatory, on its back.

In the summer of 1901 two young German sisters from Philadelphia, Hedwig (Hattie) and Bertha Pfeil, came to the seashore seeking board and summer employment.

John and Sophia Gertzen hired Hattie as a child's nurse for their young daughter Carol. Hattie became the first official tour guide of the elephant, learning her "spiel" well as she guided visitors up the six flights and making certain that they all signed the guest register. There were notable visitors such as opera and stage stars and foreign dignitaries.

One such important visitor was a young lawyer from Virginia who gave Hattie a generous tip of one dollar — the future 28th President of the United States, Woodrow Wilson.

Sophia and Hattie remained dear friends through the years in letters and cards until the death of Sophia in 1963. Hattie died in 1981 at age 93. Her story and scrapbook were given to the Save Lucy Committee by daughter Marie Kobres Bone, of Atlanta, Ga.

ELEPHANT HOTEL 65 FEET HIGH

THE MAN WHO HAS THE LARGEST ELEPHANT IN THE WORLD ON HIS HAND

JOHN GERTZEN

FINE WINES, LIQUORS AND CIGARS

MARGATE CITY, N. J.

Lucy: One of Three Sisters

Light of Asia—Cape May, NJ

Lucy the Elephant is one of three such structures designed by James V. Lafferty. It is the only one still intact. Lucy's nearest relative was the Light of Asia, a 40-foot wooden elephant built on land owned by the Neptune Land Company near the beach in what is now the Borough of South Cape May. This elephant was owned by Theodore Reger of Philadelphia and built under the supervision of James Bradley, a builder of the area. Work began on the frame in May of 1884 from plans drawn by architect N. H. Culber, also of Philadelphia.

The structure was 40 feet, 10 inches tall, or 58 feet, 2 inches to the top of the howdah. The howdah itself was 11 feet long and the elephant's trunk, which terminated in a large barrel on the ground, was 21 feet long. A wooden platform on which the elephant was based was 834 feet, 9 inches long and 40 feet wide.

It was estimated that a million pieces of wood were used in the construction, plus 250 kegs of nails and six tons of bolts. The tinsmith supplied 13,400 square feet of tin to cover the framework. Entrance was made through the hind legs and a spiral staircase led to a small concession stand inside. Refreshments were also sold from stands in the front legs of the structure.

In spite of the fact that hundreds of people arrived by excursion trains and boats to Cape May to see this oddity, it was never a financial success. Concession and admittance fees never covered the $18,000 cost of construction. The Mount Vernon Land Company became owners of the elephant in 1887 and used it for advertising a new real estate development. By the spring of 1900 the elephant had deteriorated to the point it was declared beyond saving and Capt. Samuel E. Ewing of Cape May was given a contract to tear it down. The last remains, according to newspaper reports of the day, were cremated on May 26, 1900.

Light of Asia, the Cape May Elephant. Left unattended it was finally demolished. (Circa 1890)

Elephantine Colossus—Coney Island, NY

Lucy's other relative, Elephantine Colossus, was built by James V. Lafferty at Coney Island, N.Y., as an attraction for the spot that at the time was the Disneyland of its era.

Work was started in the spring of 1884. The elephant, intended strictly as an amusement attraction, was said to have cost $65,000. It measured 122 feet in height and contained seven floors of exhibits and rooms.

Built two years before the Statue of Liberty, the Coney Island elephant caused considerable excitement. However, it was a financial loss from the beginning. From the howdah that topped the structure, visitors had an aerial view of more than 50 miles of ocean, bays and the cities of New York, Brooklyn and Jersey City.

The elephant was divided into 31 rooms, each with its own designation such as Main Hall, Shoulder Room, Throat Room, Stomach Room, etc. Sixty-five windows took care of ventilation. It was illuminated by 25 electric lights.

Overall view of the Coney Island, N.Y. elephant built by Lafferty.

Poster used for the Coney Island elephant, the original of which is in the Lucy Gift Shop.

According to notes of J.T. McCaddon, manager, the elephant contained 3,500,000 feet of lumber, 11,000 kegs of nails, 12 tons of iron bolts and is covered by 57,000 square feet of tin. It took 263 men, 129 full working days to complete.

Located on Surf Avenue, it was just across from the terminals of all the railroad and steamboat lines into Coney Island. In fact McCaddon bragged that the, "New York and Sea Beach RR runs direct to the entrance of the elephant."

Finally, Lafferty sold the structure to a Philadelphia syndicate.

The structure's worth as an attraction faded as newer ones grew up around it and competed for the visitors' dollars. From newspaper accounts of the time, it became somewhat of a run-down boarding house. By 1896 it was practically a deserted structure. On Sunday evening, September 27, 1896, the elephant building caught fire and crumbled to the sand.

The Turkish Pavilion

The Turkish Pavilion, constructed in 1876 for the Centennial Exhibition in Philadelphia's West Fairmount Park, had attracted Anthony Gertzen's eye and when it became available after the close of the fair, he purchased the building, had it disassembled into numbered sections and moved to Margate, where it was carefully restored and reconstructed behind the famous elephant.

The pavilion, now owned by his son John, with its stained glass windows near the ceiling, creating rainbows below and exotic architectures with onion-

The Turkish Pavalion was brought to the Margate site after the World's Fair in Philadelphia. It was located to the rear of the elephant for many years.

shaped domes on the roof, became a popular night club for many years. John and Sophia also acquired Gillighans, a large hotel across the street from the elephant, then operated as a gambling place with slot machines, horse race equipment, etc. They changed the name to the Mansion House and made it into a rooming house.

According to legend, Sophia Gertzen is responsible for the name "Lucy," a title that has stuck with the elephant through the years. There is no concrete story ever recorded, however, as to why the name was chosen or as coming from Sophia.

In 1902, an English doctor and his family leased the elephant as a summer home. They moved into Lucy's ample interior and converted the main hall into four bedrooms, a dining room, kitchen and parlor. A bathroom was outfitted in one of the small front shoulder closets using a miniature bathtub.

Lucy was heavily damaged in the storm of 1903 and was standing knee deep in the sand before volunteers helped to dig her out and move her farther back from the sea. Then, according to newspaper accounts, Lucy was converted into a tavern. Rowdy drinkers kept knocking over the oil lanterns used for lighting. In 1904 Lucy was nearly burned to the ground as a result of this carelessness. This ended her days as a tavern.

1900s: Many Uses for Lucy

John Gertzen died in 1916, leaving Sophia with two young children to raise and support. To add to the family income, she began a tourist camp which was to become so popular that it required 40 tents to satisfy the demand.

Others began to copy Sophia's successful venture until a "Tent City" arose along the waterfront. The City Fathers did not relish the situation and passed an ordinance banning all "habitation in tents" on the Margate beaches.

The pavilion had been leased to a family named Dougherty and operated as a "speakeasy." It was shut down when the Volstead Act of 1920 became law.

Sophia, undaunted, converted the pavilion into a rooming house and this plus her 10¢ admission to the famed elephant became her only source of income.

A guest register shows that in 1916 such notables as President and Mrs. Woodrow Wilson, Vincent and John Jacob Astor, the duPonts of Delaware, Henry Ford and even the Rajah of Bhong and his wives from Singapore all visited Lucy and climbed her steps to the howdah on her back.

In 1929 a violent storm tore off the howdah, which was later replaced by a less ornate one.

Photo of the elephant when it was used as a tourist camp. Some of the 40 tents erected there are seen in the background.

The Volstead Act (Prohibition) was repealed in 1933 and Sophia again went into the saloon business along with her two children, who were now adults. Obtaining liquor license #1 from the City of Margate, they renovated the Turkish Pavilion into an old-fashioned beer garden and re-named it the Elephant Cafe.

The popularity of the cafe continued through World War II until Sophia's advancing years prompted her to sell the cafe, but still retaining Lucy the Elephant and the family's summer home. After several owners, Sophia repurchased the Elephant Cafe and converted it into the Elephant Hotel.

In 1944 a hurricane devastated the Jersey coast. Lucy took a beating but somehow survived. Other nearby properties including the entire Margate Boardwalk were destroyed.

Sophia died in 1963 at the age of 86. Those who knew her said she had a beautiful nature and a great sense of humor.

Sophia's children Caroline Bonnelli and Joseph F. Gertzen continued to run the business, the hotel and the famous elephant Lucy as a tourist attraction, a refreshment stand, bathhouses and small rental cottages until 1970. In that year they donated Lucy to the newly-formed Save Lucy Committee, sold the land to developers and retired to Florida.

1969: Saving a Decaying Lucy

After years of neglect, Lucy was on the verge of crumbling.

In 1969, Edwin T. Carpenter and a group of Margate citizens formed the Margate Civic Association. One purpose of the Association was to find a way to save the decaying old elephant landmark from demolition, as a developer was negotiating the purchase of the land upon which Lucy stood.

The City of Margate owned a piece of vacant beachfront property two blocks west of the elephant that had been purchased in a public referendum in 1932 for recreation purposes. Mr. Carpenter and members of the association approached the City with the possibility of moving Lucy to this city parkland.

Mayor Martin Bloom and Commissioners William Ross and Russell Roney were receptive to the idea providing the city would not be held responsible for any damages that might occur. The owners were pleased to donate the elephant, hoping Lucy would be preserved, but stipulated "if it falls down" the Civic Association would be responsible for the removal of the elephant's remains.

John A. Milner, AIA, of West Chester, Pennsylvania, a nationally known restoration architect, was contacted by the Civic Association to examine the elephant structure and determine the feasibility of relocation. After careful study, Milner and his associates determined that the building was structurally sound and would survive the move.

The Committee to Save Lucy is Formed

The challenge of moving the elephant was presented to the Civic Association and thus the Save Lucy Committee was formed.

The house-moving firm of Mullen and Ranalli was hired to prepare the structure for the move at a cost of $9,000. Feriozzi & Sons, a local area concrete contractor, was hired to prepare an especially designed foundation at the new site for a cost of $15,000. These costs presented a major expenditure for the committee.

In addition to raising these sums the committee was presented with a 30-day time limit for relocation by the owners' attorney or be solely responsible for demolition and removal costs.

A series of fundraising events was planned to meet the deadline. The most successful was a house-to-house canvass by volunteers who approached every houseowner in Margate.

Mayor Bloom proclaimed June 27, 1970, as "Lucy Day." School children donated proceeds from sales of cakes and crafts to help Lucy.

In spite of all these efforts the committee was short of its goal by $10,000 as the deadline for the move approached.

Chairpersons Josephine Harron and Sylvia Carpenter signed a personal note with the help of an anonymous co-signer providing the means to proceed.

The original Committe to Save Lucy, pictured in 1970

1970: The Challenge is to Move Lucy!

The morning of July 20, 1970, was set as "Lucy moving day."
It looked like all obstacles had been removed and that the giant undertaking would proceed according to schedule.
Then came a jolt that was not anticipated.
Three days before the moving date, the Committee was served with a legal injunction to prevent the relocation of the elephant! The Atlantic Beach Corporation claimed that the presence of the giant Lucy would deflate values of property owned by this corporation adjacent to the new site. A hearing was scheduled for exactly one day after the 30-day deadline on the moving.
The movers had already installed wood cribbing under the elephant's body, raised it with special house jacks fastened to huge I beams placed on special dollies.
The Committee made a desperate appeal to Atlantic County Judge Benjamin Rimm, who agreed to hold an unprecedented Saturday morning hearing in the County Courtroom.

Lucy procession moves down Atlantic Avenue as hundreds watch. (Photo by Charles McKee.)

After listening to arguments from both sides, Judge Rimm dissolved the injunction and ruled in favor of the Save Lucy Committee.

There was little time for rejoicing and celebrating because preparations that had been halted had to be resumed at a fevered pace. Workmen labored around the clock Saturday night and Sunday, finally announcing everything was ready.

On Monday, July 20, 1970 everyone was assembled at the Lucy site by 7:00 a.m. Last minute inspection showed all was well and ready for the "go ahead" signal, just as a heavy fog rolled in!

There was frantic checking with the weather bureau as workmen, the news media and the committee stood about drinking coffee. The weather had been predicted for perfect conditions just the day before.

At 9:00 a.m. a welcome breeze sprung up and the fog started to clear to the cheers and relief of everyone present

A few minutes after nine, the foreman shouted "Let 'er roll," blew his whistle and one of the strangest processions ever witnessed in New Jersey began.

A small pickup truck began pulling the giant elephant in a half circle toward the curb on Cedar Grove Avenue. The massive structure creaked and groaned as it was eased over the curb and turned onto Atlantic Avenue.

The small truck leading the slow march was dwarfed by Lucy's size and brought forth comments from spectators such as, "Does it have the power to tow this six-story, 90-ton structure?"

The answer was: it did!

Squads of police, car lights flashing, stood by as Atlantic City Electric Company and New Jersey Bell Telephone Company linemen dropped power, telephone and cable lines to allow the giant to pass safely. The proud Save Lucy Committee and thousands of spectators cheered and applauded.

Albert Ranalli, a partner in the firm of Mullen and Ranalli of Mount Holly, N.J. was overall director of the project. Spectators said he was a combination of suspense and silent prayer. He told reporters: "This is the most unusual moving job we have ever been asked to perform or, for that matter, envision. The only thing that could equal it would be to move the Sphinx from the Valley of the Nile."

Margate Mayor Bloom, City Commissioners and officials of other municipalities attended the moving. Bloom's comment was: "You had to see it to believe it. For a lady ninety years old, it is marvelous that she could stand such a rigorous ordeal."

TV crews from all the major networks filmed the slow but majestic march, while newspaper cameras clicked to capture the scene for posterity.

After approximately seven hours, Lucy was safely tied down in her new location. It was a tired, but happy crew and committee that finally decided to call it a day. There was much celebrating at both private and public parties.

Lucy moves to her new home.

Atlantic City Press photo by Mike Blizzard (used by special permission).

The Next Challenge

Once Lucy was firmly anchored in her new location, repaying the loan for the move and financing the restoration became the next challenge of the Save Lucy Committee. The publicity of moving the giant Lucy went over the national and international wire services, creating a flow of donations to the Save Lucy Committee from world-wide good-wishers.

The Atlantic City Race Course offered the Committee a "Lucy Day at the Races" with all profits going to Lucy. Atlantic City's 500 Club, with its famous headliners, offered the Committee a gala night. School children and teachers held events and chipped in. One class sent their end-of-year treasury of 67¢.

Although these efforts were helpful, it was necessary to seek larger sums in the form of corporate or government grants for historic preservation.

To accomplish this, the Save Lucy Committee applied for and received a New Jersey nonprofit corporate status and was declared a tax-deductible entity under the Internal Revenue Code.

On September 8, 1971 Lucy's application for recognition on the National Register of Historic Places was announced from Washington, D.C., opening doors for State and Federal matching grants.

The architectural firm of John A. Milner began drawings for Phase I, stabilization of the structure, and Phase II, historic preservation. The cost was estimated to be $124,000.

The first grant award from the Historic Preservation program of the Department of Housing and Urban Development was in the sum of $61,750 half of the architect's estimated costs.

Committee President Josephine Harron and Vice President Sylvia Carpenter, on advice of an area advertising executive, arranged for a unique type of loan, having 62 sponsors, who pledged to borrow $1,000 each from a local bank. They would pay the interest for a five-year period while the committee would repay the loan principal. Some donated the full pledge. Through this means the committee would be able to match the grant and start work on the restoration.

Locating a contractor who would tackle the job proved quite a task, as several turned it down as "impossible." Finally Arthur R. Henry of Northfield, N.J., offered to accept the challenge.

Herbert Sanford, an area carpenter turned dock builder, was assigned as foreman to handle the project. Even he was uncertain as to whether it would be successful due to the general deterioration of the structure. He called upon his friend Sam Burns to come out of retirement to help him. Together they formulated the basic plan for the restoration and work began in 1973.

The $124,000 raised for total restoration melted away rapidly. It became necessary to insert structural steel to replace the main trusses that were in worse condition than first believed, which escalated the cost considerably. The threading of the steel beams through two 12-inch holes in the rump of the elephant proved to be a very tedious operation.

Other problems also appeared and it soon became apparent that the estimated cost was not realistic and additional funds would be needed.

Replacing Lucy's metal skin and reconstructing the Victorian-designed howdah were still in the future.

1974: Lucy Re-Opens!

The work accomplished with the $124,000 was sufficient to permit tours inside Lucy to begin again by summer of 1974. The Committee members acted as guides. A ribbon cutting ceremony was held with the mayor and city commissioners attending and press stories went out on the wire services: "LUCY THE MARGATE ELEPHANT OPEN FOR TOURS."

The Committee again applied for help from HUD in 1975. They also filed applications with the Department of the Interior's National Park Service and the New Jersey Office of Historic Sites. A New Jersey State matching grant was awarded first and work on Lucy's metal hide began. The matching HUD grant was still being processed when the contractor informed the Committee he could not stop work of applying the metal while waiting for approval, because the building would deteriorate further and work already accomplished would be in jeopardy.

This was a very generous offer and the committee accepted, not realizing it would become involved in more governmental red tape on account of the decision. The HUD office in Washington, discovering that the skin had been completely applied, refused to release the grant, pointing out it was against its policy to pay for work already accomplished.

After a few trips to Washington and with the help of New Jersey legislative representatives, the committee proved that no guidelines had been established for this particular program and that the committee had notified HUD on several occasions that they were proceeding with the metal skin application to avoid jeopardizing the restoration work already accomplished. The grant was finally released, but the contractor waited several months before the committee could pay him.

The restoration of Lucy's exterior took almost three years to complete due to financing delays and escalating construction costs.

Lucy was enjoying her second year of visitors, one of whom was sailing on an ocean trip to the New York Harbor to see the "Tall Ships" arrive. Upon sighting the elephant he decided to moor his ship at the Atlantic City Marina and taxi to Margate with his family for a tour of the famous Lucy. He later introduced himself as Irenee du Pont, Jr. from Wilmington, Del. and made the fantastic and generous offer to donate a very sophisticated fire suppression system for inside Lucy's wooden body, similar to the kind used in museums and computer rooms. One of the committee's main concerns had always been fear of fire and this was like a gift from heaven. While on the tour inside Lucy, he had recognized his sisters' and cousins' names on an old 1916 guest register. They had been visiting their grandmother who owned a summer home in the neighboring Ventnor City.

1974 visitors welcomed for tours.

> **LUCY, THE MARGATE ELEPHANT**
> has been designated a
> **NATIONAL
> HISTORIC LANDMARK**
> This site possesses national significance
> in commemorating the history of the
> **UNITED STATES OF AMERICA**
> National Park Service
> United States Department of the Interior

Copy of plaque designating Lucy as a historical landmark.

By 1976 Lucy's metal skin and new ornate howdah were in place and freshly painted. The U.S. Department of the Interior recognized Lucy as a National Historic Landmark, taking her place alongside of Independence Hall, the Alamo and other famous sites that possess national significance in commemorating the history of the United States of America.

Presentation of National Landmark plaque by Eugene Peluso, landmark coordinator for the National Park Service, Deptartment of the Interior.

Crowd gathers to watch workers put finishing touches to the Lucy reconstruction at Decatur Avenue and the beach.

For the Bicentennial celebration of 1976, the Committee arranged for a series of free summer concerts on an outdoor bandstand erected especially for the occasion. These concerts drew big crowds and were so successful they have been continued each summer.

When the former Elephant Hotel and outlying buildings were being demolished to make way for a condominium at Lucy's old site, the committee was able to secure a small building formerly used by the Camden and Atlantic Railroad in the 1880s. It was moved and renovated to become the first gift shop on the Lucy grounds. Eventually a two story addition to the little railroad depot was constructed by volunteers, improving the size of the shop and creating an office and badly needed storage area on the second floor. Business was growing with more and more visitors.

A Victorian wrought iron fence was purchased by the City of Margate and erected around Lucy's historic park by the U.S. Army Reserves "C" Co. 469th Engineers, "STORCK" Reserve Center, Northfield, N.J. and members of the local iron workers union.

In 1980-81, the Office of New Jersey Heritage awarded a matching grant of $48,000 to begin the interior restoration. Resorts International Casino offered the Committee the chance to sell tickets to the Lou Rawls show to help match the grant. Many other fund raisers were scheduled until the committee finally matched the grant one year later. The state funds did not become

New refreshment pavilion opened in 1987.

available until the entire cost of $96,000 was expended, forcing the committee again to borrow thousands before reimbursement.

Through a New Jersey Green Acres loan of $100,000 the Lucy Committee has been able to construct a Victorian-designed refreshment pavilion, relocate and rebuild the bandstand and add some much needed shrubbery.

The annual income from the gift shop and tours has covered operating costs, but has not provided sufficient funds to pursue future plans or cover the maintenance costs of repainting Lucy, which averages $25,000 every two or three years. The anticipated income from the refreshment pavilion is expected to overcome these needs.

The Save Lucy Committee, Inc. now numbers over 40 members, who act as volunteers. Millions of hours have been donated by these dedicated people who are sincere in their love for this once forsaken structure.

This history of Lucy has been the history of the dedicated Gertzen family who once owned Lucy for 80-odd years and the Committee, who since 1969 has accomplished almost unbelievable feats in selling the picturesque Margate elephant to the City, the State and the Nation.

To date, the Save Lucy Committee has, by its own efforts, raised more than $1.5 million to reserve for future generations this unique architectural wonder of the Victorian era, which will never be forgotten as long as Lucy continues her eternal watch over the waves of the Margate beach.

IN APPRECIATION

No history such as this could have been completed without the help of many people and organizations, library reference departments, family scrapbooks and public documents. To those sincere folk and fans of Lucy who aided this endeavor, we want to express gratitude for their interest and support.

We would especially like to thank Mary Lafferty Garrison for providing us with some previously unattainable James V. Lafferty background and photos, to Josephine (Mrs. Henry) Gertzen for her history notes on the Gertzen family, to Richard Alexander of Wynnewood for permission to quote from his Cape May Geographic Society Bulletin on Cape May's elephant "Light of Asia," the Press of Atlantic City for allowing use of an unusual photo of Lucy on her way to her new home snapped by the late photographer Mike Blizzard, to Jack E. Boucher, historian and photographer, for his early researches of the Lucy legend, Josephine Harron and Sylvia Carpenter for preparing the Committee's 18 year history of Lucy's restoration, G. Roland Brown, City Clerk 1964 1977, for his chronological history of the City of Margate and Lucy, Joseph F. (Bud) Gertzen for family and memorabilia photographs. To Bertram A. Whittaker and Norma Boice Ciszek for providing old photos from a South Atlantic City souvenir booklet and the many others who in one way or another contributed to the Lucy story.

Interior view of Lucy showing an old fire apparatus of the Margate Fire Department on display.

Partially restored interior of Main Hall of Lucy showing some of the exhibits on display.

THE SAVE LUCY COMMITTEE, INC.
2021-2022
Officers, Board of Trustees, and Staff

Josephine L. Harron, Chairman Emeritus *
Edwin T. Carpenter, Co-Founder †
Sylvia Carpenter, Co-Founder *
Davida Ross, President
Jason R. Tell, Vice President
Robert K. McGuigan, Treasurer & Chief Financial Officer
Christopher T. Hartney, Secretary & Risk Management Officer
Beth Ammazzalorso, Trustee
Commissioner John Amodeo, Trustee
Jon Ashner, Trustee
Dr. James Brady, Trustee
Susan Breitinger Gormley, Trustee
Vicki Gold Levi, Trustee
Eli Lichtenstein, Trustee
Brittany D. Middleman, Trustee
Nick Palmisano, Trustee
Martin Ross, Trustee
Bill Subin, Trustee
Petie Subin, Trustee
Joseph Wilson, Trustee

Richard D. Helfant, Executive Director & Chief Executive Officer
Jeremy E. Bingaman, Director of Education & Chief Operating Officer

Restoration Architect
Margaret Westfield, RA

General Counsel
Christopher Stanchina, Esq.

*Deceased
† Retired

PGIL2021USA